EAST ANGLIA AND THE EAST COAST RAILWAYS

THE LATE 1940s TO LATE 1960s

Brian Reading and Ian Reading

AMBERLEY

First published 2020

Amberley Publishing
The Hill, Stroud
Gloucestershire, GL5 4EP

www.amberley-books.com

ISBN 978 1 4456 9966 0 (print)
ISBN 978 1 4456 9967 7 (ebook)

British Library Cataloguing in Publication Data.
A catalogue record for this book is available from the British Library.

Origination by Amberley Publishing.
Printed in the UK.

Introduction

The 1950s and 1960s was an era of post-war renewal and change. From nationalisation in 1948 to the introduction of diesel traction in the 1960s, Britain's railways mirrored the wider cultural and technological changes taking place in society.

With pictures and recollections, heading south from York, we tour the East Coast Main Line and explore the routes of East Anglia between 1948 and 1968.

In the early 1950s, British Railways (BR) worked to overcome maintenance and staffing challenges, doing their best to return to pre-war standards. While some sheds continued to struggle, many were able to maintain their fleet of locomotives in excellent condition. With a spirit of renewal, modern BR standard steam designs were introduced, building on the best practice of earlier classes. By the late 1950s though, the era of diesel traction was fast-approaching. Waning management interest in steam delivered dire consequences. Post-war pride gave way to neglect. With flaking paint and poor maintenance, once-gleaming locomotives became shabby. Meeting the same fate as time-served locomotives, the BR standard fleet were broken-up for scrap after only a few years of service.

After more than 100 years, the end for steam was close. Galvanised by the realisation that engineering heritage could be lost forever, enthusiasts banded together with heroic railway workers to preserve memories, pictures, and at least some locomotives for future generations.

With images revealing twenty years of change, we glimpse over 150 locomotives from forty-three classes at more than forty locations.

Colour pictures were taken with a Kodak Retinette IB camera using Kodachrome slide-film, evolving from the grainy and not very colour-fast K-11 process in the 1950s, to the excellent K-12 process from the mid-1960s. Early monochrome images were produced with 116 negatives and were taken with a Kodak Box Brownie 2A in the late 1940s. An Ensign Selfix with a Ross f3.8 lens was used with 120 film from the early 1950s with much improved results. Film was scanned and digitally restored by the authors.

Pictures are arranged in six sequences:

i) following the East Coast Main Line (ECML) south from York to London.
ii) touring the East Suffolk with a trip from London to Great Yarmouth.
iii) Norwich and surrounding branch lines.
iv) visiting March shed, Lincoln and New Holland.
v) travelling on the Midland and Great Northern (M&GN) from Great Yarmouth to King's Lynn.
vi) finally, we visit a few of East Anglia's survivors as they make their way into preservation.

The East Coast Main Line (ECML) was well-engineered with many opportunities for fast running. The section south of Stoke Tunnel was a famous racing ground; well known for the exploits of Gresley's Pacific classes. Stoke bank was the venue for the record-breaking run by *Mallard* in 1938.

The first set of pictures begins at York and heads south along the ECML, with pauses at Doncaster and Grantham before photographing trackside, by the water troughs, at Werrington. The sequence continues to Peterborough, and its nearby New England shed, terminating at London King's Cross.

In contrast to the ECML's high-speed course, the former Great Eastern Railway (GER) lines from London Liverpool Street to Norwich and Great Yarmouth followed the contours of the landscape.

The East Suffolk line was a particular favourite, branching from the Great Eastern main line at Ipswich, heading for Beccles and Great Yarmouth. Remarkably, Great Yarmouth had three main stations, a further two passing stations and two halts situated on its outskirts!

Seldom far from the coast, the East Suffolk route to Great Yarmouth crossed several river valleys. With a gradient profile like the teeth of a saw and many speed restrictions, the East Suffolk was a challenging route. Weight constraints and turntable lengths prohibited the use of larger motive power for many years. However, locomotive work was often of a high standard. In the GER-era, the daily exploits of the modestly powered Claud Hamilton class 4-4-0s, with the heavy Continental Expresses to Parkeston Quay, and the North Norfolk Coast Express non-stop from Liverpool Street to North Walsham, were legendary.

Various restrictions, such as clearances around Liverpool Street, made it difficult for the LNER to make dramatic improvements after grouping. The introduction of Gresley Class B17 locomotives contributed only a modest advance over the GER 1500s (LNER Class B12). Major acceleration was not possible until the introduction of the BR standard 7MT Britannia class in 1951. In the 1950s improvements were also made to the standard of the permanent way; timetables were recast, with the Liverpool Street to Norwich service being the main beneficiary, schedules were shortened, and a regular interval-service was introduced.

While the Great Eastern main line from London Liverpool Street to Norwich continues to serve travellers, much of the East Suffolk and its branches have vanished. The Great Yarmouth to Beccles line closed in 1959; 100 years after its 1859 opening. The closure of Yarmouth South Town in 1970 left Yarmouth Vauxhall as Great Yarmouth's only remaining station.

Travelling north and east from London Liverpool Street, the second picture sequence includes suburban services at Hackney Downs and Chingford, a visit to Clacton, then onwards to Belstead Bank, Ipswich and the water troughs near Halifax Junction. Branching to the East Suffolk, the sequence takes in scenes around Beccles, St Olaves and Haddiscoe, arriving finally at Yarmouth South Town.

The third sequence begins at Norwich Thorpe station, touring the shed before taking in the spectacle of accelerating trains at Trowse and a group of GWR locomotives far from home. Other locations include Brundall, East Dereham, Swaffham and Thetford.

A fourth sequence tours March shed, glimpsing *Britannia* at Lincoln, and finally capturing the last days of BR paddle steamers at New Holland, before the building of the Humber Bridge.

The Midland and Great Northern (M&GN) line connected East Anglia's coastal towns to King's Lynn and onwards to the English Midlands. Jointly owned by the Midland Railway and the Great Northern Railway (LMS & LNER after 1923 grouping), it was managed by the LNER from 1936 until nationalisation in 1948.

Joint ownership provided the M&GN with a fascinating array of motive power representing former LMS and LNER traditions. The M&GN picture sequence begins at Yarmouth Beach and continues to Caister and South Lynn, pictured on the day that most of the line closed in 1959.

A section of the M&GN at Sheringham is preserved as the North Norfolk Railway (NNR). In the final picture sequence, we glimpse two favourite NNR locomotives as they are rescued for future generations and take in scenes of *Oliver Cromwell* being moved to Bressingham. Fittingly, the sequence concludes with *Flying Scotsman* standing beside Bill Harvey; the Norwich shed master who did so much to inspire and support the preservation movement.

As with most railway photographers our authors had their favourite locations. We hope the range of illustrations will bring back memories for those who lived through the steam era and inspire the imagination and curiosity of those who enjoy preserved railways today.

Finally, we would like to thank local railway historian Richard Adderson for his generous assistance and the Amberley team for their support and encouragement.

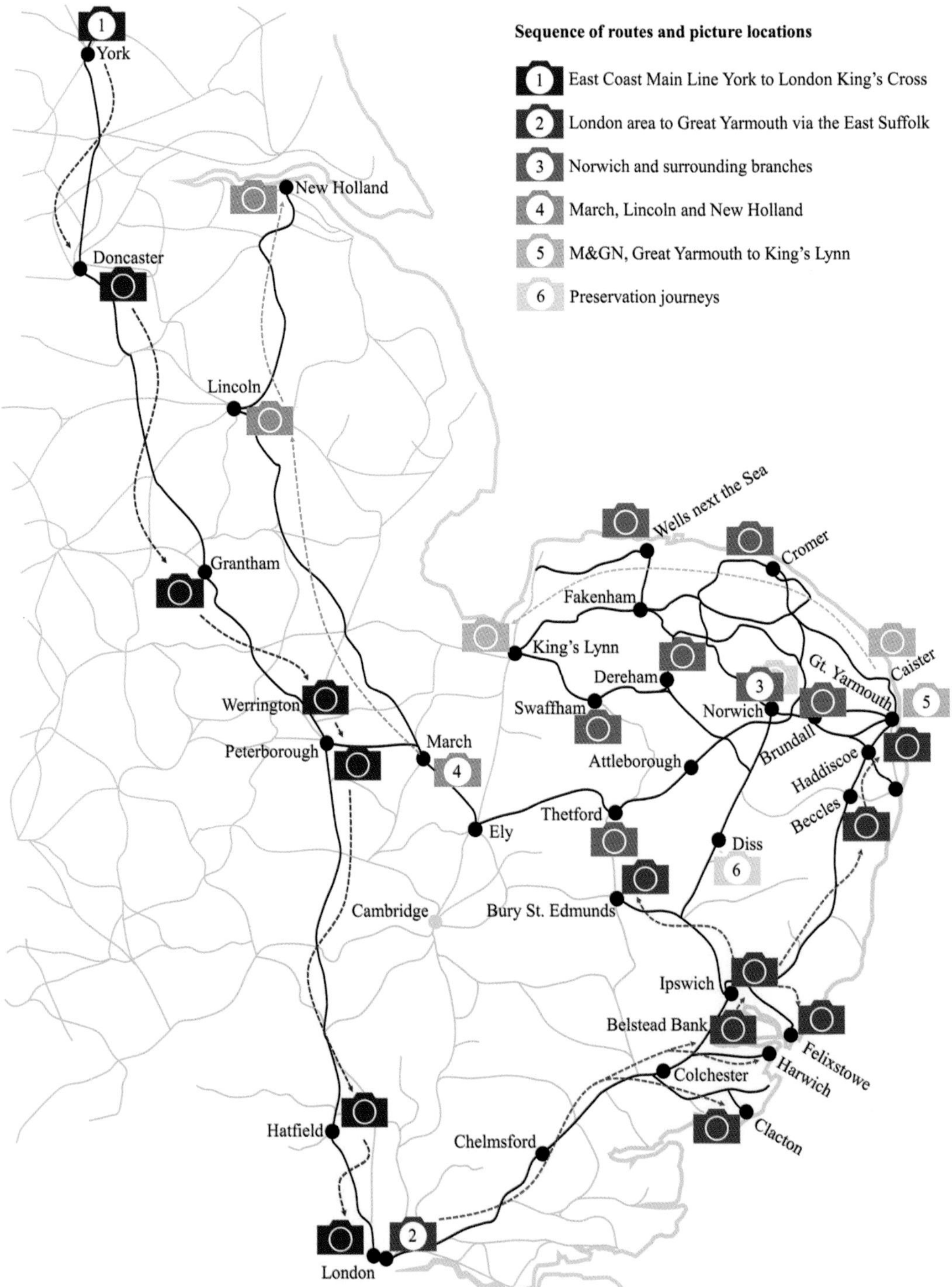
Sequence of routes and picture locations
1 East Coast Main Line York to London King's Cross
2 London area to Great Yarmouth via the East Suffolk
3 Norwich and surrounding branches
4 March, Lincoln and New Holland
5 M&GN, Great Yarmouth to King's Lynn
6 Preservation journeys
York
New Holland
Doncaster
Lincoln
Grantham
Werrington
Peterborough
March
Ely
Cambridge
Hatfield
London
Chelmsford
Colchester
Clacton
Harwich
Felixstowe
Ipswich
Belstead Bank
Bury St. Edmunds
Thetford
Diss
Attleborough
Swaffham
Dereham
King's Lynn
Fakenham
Wells next the Sea
Cromer
Norwich
Brundall
Gt. Yarmouth
Caister
Haddiscoe
Beccles

East Coast Main Line York to London King's Cross

The road to the north from York, 1961. An A4 gets away nicely with a train for Edinburgh. The record-breaking Class A4 will forever be remembered as the masterpiece of its designer Sir Nigel Gresley.

Class B16/3 No. 61434 passes York on the southbound through road, June 1960. The B16/3 was a 1949 Thompson rebuild of the North Eastern Railway Raven S3. Thompson's design replaced Raven's Stephenson valve gear with three sets of Walschaerts valve gear. Earlier, Gresley had rebuilt seven of the S3 class with his conjugated valve gear for the middle cylinder as B16/2.

June 1960, Gresley A3 No. 60055 *Woolwinder*, on the southbound through road at York, with a Newcastle to London King's Cross express. Note the small smoke deflectors; they were fitted to some Class A3 locomotives before the large German type became standard.

Seen in June 1960, in the usual beautifully clean condition for this working, Class A4 No. 60032 *Gannet* heads 'the Elizabethan' through York. Named in 1953 to mark the coronation of Queen Elizabeth II, by 1954 the service was achieving over 60 mph average from London King's Cross to Edinburgh. 'The Elizabethan' was the longest scheduled non-stop service in the world.

June 1960. The corresponding southbound up working of this famous train runs through York with Gresley A4 No. 60027 *Merlin* at the head. This A4 spent her working life allocated to Scottish sheds, most of the time at Haymarket. The boiler-side plaque relates to H.M.S. *Merlin*, the Royal Naval Air Station, at Donibristle in Fife.

A nicely turned out Gresley A3, No. 60044 *Melton* brings a London King's Cross to Newcastle train into York. By June 1960, the draughting on the locomotive has been modified with a Kylchap double chimney; the German-style smoke deflectors are yet to be added.

June 1960, Gresley A3 No. 60071 *Tranquil* runs through York on the northbound 'Anglo-Scottish Car Carrier'. Passengers loaded their cars onto special rolling-stock, travelling in comfort by train, and avoiding the long drive to Scotland.

BR standard Class 7 No. 70002 *Geoffrey Chaucer* rumbles south through Doncaster with an up freight in the mid-1960s. The Britannia class were the first of the BR standard locomotives, drawing on best practice from the former railway companies.

Doncaster, 1961, Peppercorn Class A1, No. 60120 *Kittiwake*, pauses with a southbound up Pullman. Unusually, for a Pullman service, the train does not have a headboard. Either somebody forgot, or the locomotive was a last-minute substitute.

Disappointing condition for a Gresley Pacific with a badly scorched smokebox door. Gresley A3 No. 60088 *Book Law* passes Doncaster with a southbound up express. Spotters enjoy the spectacle, conscientiously recording the number.

Pictured at Doncaster, Thompson B1 No. 61087 starts away with empty stock. The train terminated at Doncaster and is now moving off towards the yards. The crew have changed the headlamp code whilst the passengers were alighting.

Looking shabby, but speeding through the haze of steam and smoke, Gresley V2 No. 60837 heads south through Doncaster with an up express. Scorch marks on the smokebox door usually indicated hard work and poor ash removal.

Britannia No. 70036 *Boadicea* was introduced in 1952, and spent her early years based at Stratford and Norwich. By the mid-1960s, she is seen working on the East Coast Main Line, running northbound into Doncaster.

Peppercorn A1 No. 60157 *Great Eastern* brings a southbound up express into the platform at Doncaster. *Great Eastern* was one of several A1 class members named after former railway companies; her nameplate includes the Great Eastern Railway crest.

Summer Saturdays saw Gresley K3 locomotives regularly pressed into service on passenger trains. Hull-based No. 61985 arrives in the Doncaster up main platform. This was possibly an extra service, complete with reporting number on the top lamp bracket.

Thompson A2/3 No. 60523 *Sun Castle* leaving Doncaster with a London King's Cross to Leeds train. The forty locomotives of Class A2 had varied beginnings. Thompson rebuilt all six members of the Gresley P2 (2-8-2) class as A2/2 (4-6-2) and amended an order for four Gresley V2 (2-6-2) locomotives as A2/1 (4-6-2). Fifteen new A2/3 class were constructed before Thompson's retirement. Fifteen more were later built to the more visually pleasing Peppercorn A2 design. Double chimneys were later fitted to several members of the class.

Grantham, early 1960s; Peppercorn A1 No. 60139 *Sea Eagle* starts a northbound express. The locomotive had just recovered from a violent bout of slipping. The driver looked down, smiled at me, and said; 'I reckon that was there before I started!'

Grantham 1961; Gresley A3 No. 60039 *Sandwich* pulls away with an up express for London King's Cross. Built in 1934 at Doncaster, *Sandwich* was named after Lord Rosebery's racehorse, winner of the 1931 St Leger at Doncaster Racecourse.

Pictured by the up platform at Grantham in the 1950s, Gresley A4 No. 60022 *Mallard* pauses with a Newcastle to London King's Cross express. The boiler-side plaque commemorates her 3 July 1938 speed record of 126 mph. No. 60022 (4468) is preserved and displayed at the National Railway Museum in York.

Class L1 No. 67745 stands in the bay platform at Grantham with a train ready to leave for Nottingham. Designed by the LNER under Thompson, all except one of this class of 100 were built after the formation of British Railways. With relatively small 5-foot 2-inch driving wheels, the L1 class suffered from mechanical wear at higher speeds.

Werrington north of Peterborough; four tracks of the East Coast Main Line beside the double track of the Peterborough to Midlands route. Gresley A4 No. 60031 *Golden Plover* speeds south with a Saturday service. Carrying a reversed headboard, the locomotive will probably have worked a weekday non-stop to Edinburgh the day before.

Members of Peppercorn's A1 class were also very visible on the East Coast Main Line. August 1960, Werrington, No. 60120 *Kittiwake* heads north with 'the Queen of Scots' Pullman.

The black zigzag-sign marks the location of the water troughs at Werrington. Gresley A4 No. 60003 *Andrew K. McCosh*, *c.* 1960, northbound picking up water at speed.

Gresley A3 No. 60105 *Victor Wild* heads south with an up express at Werrington. The locomotive has received the draughting improvements – Kylchap double chimney and German-style smoke deflectors – that became standard for the class.

The Gresley V2 class were competent locomotives that were used extensively for express passenger work as well as mixed-traffic and fast freight. No. 60903 heads north at Werrington in July 1960 with an empty stock working. The first two coaches are an articulated set, a number of these were introduced by the LNER in the 1930s.

The up slow line at Werrington accommodates a Class J6 heading south with a mixed freight. Introduced by the Great Northern Railway in 1911; the J6 class was designed by Henry Ivatt. His son, George Ivatt, became well known as an innovating LMS chief mechanical engineer. No. 64206 is pictured in August 1960 perhaps performing one of her last duties. Sadly, she was withdrawn just weeks later in September 1960.

Thompson B1 No. 61367 heads north at Werrington on the slow line with a ballast train. The train is equipped with plenty of brake vans!

Peterborough New England shed is hosting Gresley A3 No. 60036 *Colombo*, not in a particularly good state of cleanliness. The locomotive has received a Kylchap double chimney, but smoke deflectors are yet to be added.

Class J50/3 keeps company with a former War Department Austerity 2-8-0 at Peterborough New England. Pictured *c.* 1960, No. 68976 was built in 1930 by the LNER as a continuation of a Gresley Great Northern design.

BR standard 9F 2-10-0 No. 92036 in front of a former Great Northern Railway J6 0-6-0. Both rest beside Peterborough New England shed *c.* 1960. A Riddles design, No. 92036 was introduced in 1954. At nearly 140 tons she's a giant beside the 50-ton J6. Although the 9F has nearly twice the tractive effort of her vintage companion, it's interesting to speculate whether, in her ten-year life, she came close to hauling the total tonnage of the already nearly fifty-year-old J6.

Left: Gresley A3 No. 60044 *Melton*, in good condition, stands under the coaling tower at Peterborough New England. The photograph shows the German-style smoke deflectors and Kylchap double chimney fitted to the class in their final years.

Below: Gresley V2 No. 60880 at Peterborough stands by to cover for any locomotive failures on this summer Saturday. Seen in 1961, illuminated by a low sun, she has recently been fitted with a double chimney.

Peppercorn A1 No. 60123 *H.A. Ivatt* runs into Peterborough with an express for the north. Before steam faded, locomotives on major East Coast Main Line services were kept clean. No. 60123 is named after Henry Alfred Ivatt, the chief mechanical engineer of the Great Northern Railway and father of the other famous Ivatt, Henry George.

BR standard Class 4 4-6-0 No. 75043 stands at the Peterborough southbound up platform. The picture shows Peterborough before the major alterations were made in the 1970s.

Ivatt 4MT No. 43082 at Peterborough. Boxes and trolleys on the platform are a reminder of the railway's significant parcels business. Vans and open wagons in the background illustrate that freight traffic was still thriving in the 1950s.

Thompson A2/3 No. 60513 *Dante* pauses at Peterborough with a London King's Cross train. *Dante* is pictured, *c.* 1960, while she was based at Peterborough New England shed.

Ivatt 4MT No. 43151, with express head-code, is probably adding a van to a passenger train. The pickup freight was still a feature of the railways. Passenger trains often had freight vans added for portions of their journey.

In the early 1960s, Peppercorn A1 No. 60123 *H.A. Ivatt* pulls away from Peterborough. She is passed by a southbound train headed by an A4, also in lovely condition. This period of the East Coast Main Line represented steam running at its best with schedules gradually being improved.

Thompson A2/3 No. 60513 *Dante* eases forward past Peterborough North signal box, ready to take a train to London King's Cross.

Gresley A4 No. 60007 *Sir Nigel Gresley* follows the A2/3 on the same mission, running forward to pick up a working for London King's Cross. In later years, it was very unusual to change locomotives at this station, but there were some workings that originated from Peterborough.

Right: Gresley A4 No. 60007 *Sir Nigel Gresley* prepares to leave Peterborough for London King's Cross. The 100th Pacific constructed by the GNR and LNER, named in honour of her designer, No. 60007 (4498) is preserved and maintained in running condition.

Below: Thompson B1 No. 61143 is passing under the East Coast Main Line in the 1960s, near Peterborough East station, with a summer Saturday express for East Anglia.

July 1951 – Peppercorn A1 No. 60124 *Kenilworth* heads through Potters Bar bound for London King's Cross.

A smoky scene at London King's Cross Top Shed in 1957. Gresley A4 No. 60015 *Quicksilver*, in the foreground, is still with original chimney and blast arrangement. She was fitted with a double chimney weeks later in August 1957.

Gresley N2 class No. 69506 and No. 69525 at rest at London King's Cross Top Shed in 1957. Both locomotives are fitted with condensing gear for working the underground section to Moorgate.

Gresley A3 No. 60096 *Papyrus*, fresh from post-war overhaul, waits to depart with an express for the north. Gresley rolling stock is still in use; British Railways Mk I coaches were introduced a few years later in 1951.

Gresley V2 No. 60813, *c.* 1948, about to leave London King's Cross. The locomotive has received small smoke deflectors around a modified chimney. The Gresley teak coaches in the background still carry LNER lettering. The poster suggests Gracie Fields is performing in London.

London Area to Great Yarmouth via the East Suffolk

With a servicing depot as part of the station complex, the sweet smell of steam and smoke was always in the air at London Liverpool Street. On 30 July 1951, Gresley/Thompson B2 No. 61644 *Earlham Hall* lines up with Thompson B1 No. 61098 eager to depart. An electric train is visible in the background. Overhead cables in this era ran only to Shenfield.

With the B1 on her way, B2 No. 61644 *Earlham Hall* is revealed as she prepares to leave for Clacton. The LNER Chief Mechanical Engineer Edward Thompson began rebuilding the Gresley B17 class with two instead of three cylinders. Nine were rebuilt from 1945 to 1947, a tenth in 1949. With boiler pressure reduced to ease maintenance, the remaining B17 locomotives were outperformed by Thompson's ten B2 rebuilds. Later reboilered and operated to 225 psi, the remaining B17 fleet regained its performance-edge. No more were rebuilt.

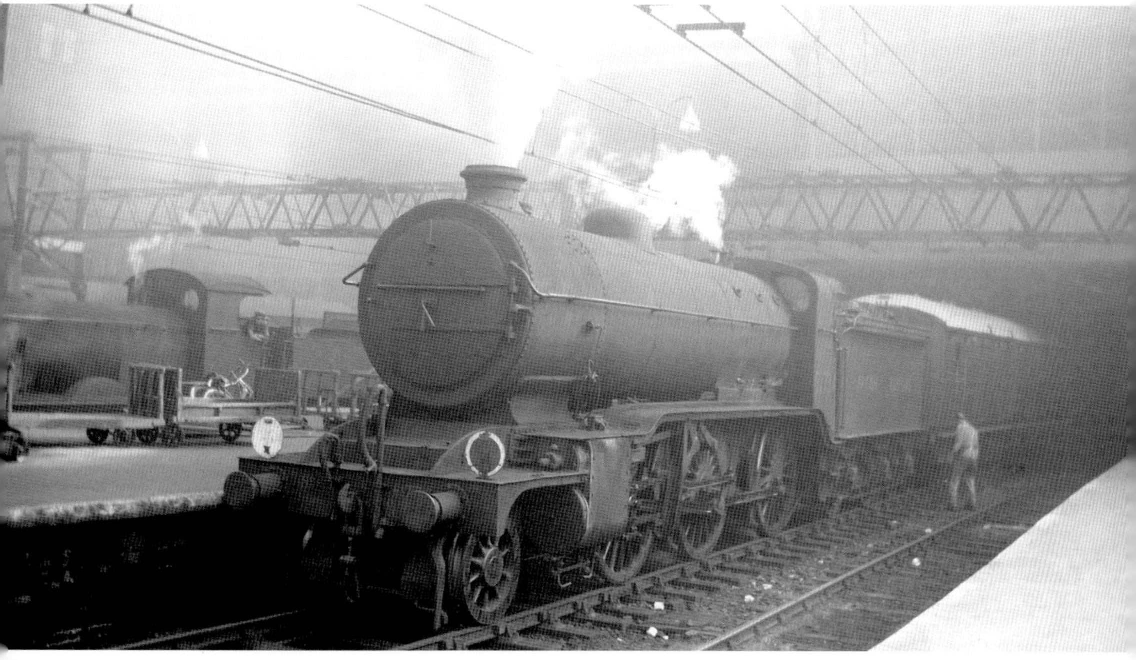

Gresley K2 No. 61734 waits at typically smoky London Liverpool Street, *c.* 1949. Responding to a shortage of larger express passenger locomotives, some of these Great Northern Railway (GNR) 2-6-0 locomotives were allocated to the Great Eastern section after the formation of the LNER. As more members of Class B12, and later Class B17 became available, the situation was eased, but many of the GNR intruders remained. White coach roofs look like an effort to regain pre-war styling. The J15 in the background is unusual, perhaps filling in for one of the station pilots.

Class B2 No. 61614 *Castle Hedingham* at London Liverpool Street. Released from her Clacton arrival, she waits before reversing to the nearby locomotive yard for servicing. During the 1950s the B2 class were deployed on Clacton interval services. Most were allocated to Colchester, working also from the Clacton sub-shed.

BR standard Britannia 7MT No. 70002 *Geoffrey Chaucer* arrives at London Liverpool Street with the up 'Broadsman' from Norwich. The picture dates from the 1950s when No. 70002 was allocated to Stratford; shed code 30A.

A Class N7 runs smartly into Hackney Downs with a London Liverpool Street suburban service. Known locally as the 'Jazz Service', it was said to be the most intensive steam-hauled service in the world. With a timetable expressed in half-minutes, the schedule depended on extremely tight turnaround times at Liverpool Street during rush hours. Overhead cables are a reminder that the locomotive's days are numbered. No. 69636 was withdrawn in 1960.

Chingford on a wet day during the last few months of the steam-operated Jazz Service. N7 No. 69693, and one of her class mates, are being coaled. Railway work often involved hard work in poor conditions with basic tools.

Class B2 No. 61615 *Culford Hall* leaves Clacton in the 1950s with a London Liverpool Street interval service. Nine of the ten B17 class-members rebuilt to Class B2 had their smaller Great Eastern tenders replaced. Most received second-hand North Eastern Railway (NER) units. No. 61615 was one of two to receive tenders from withdrawn Class P1 2-8-2 locomotives. P1 tenders were modified to remove the booster previously mounted at the front.

A busy summer Saturday scene at Clacton in the early 1950s. There is plenty going on in the background with J20 No. 64682 and D16/3 No. 62543 visible. Class B2 No. 61614 *Castle Hedingham* arrives with a cross-country train of holiday makers. This B2 received an ex-NER tender when it was rebuilt from a Class B17.

July 1951, B2 No. 61632 *Belvoir Castle* has brought her train into Clacton from London Liverpool Street. Easing forward, she will use the engine release road to run to the locomotive shed for servicing. The locomotive is one of two from Class B2 that received tenders from withdrawn Class P1. Most B2 locomotives received B1-pattern smokebox doors. No. 61632 has retained her B17 door. When B2 No. 61671 *Royal Sovereign* was withdrawn in 1958 for a few months, No. 61632 was renamed *Royal Sovereign* to take her place as the official royal engine.

Ivatt Class 2MT No. 46466 rests near Clacton shed. 2MTs were used occasionally on cross-country services from Cambridge, joining the main line at Marks Tey then branching at Colchester for the line to Clacton.

For many years a train ferry operated from Harwich to Zeebrugge. It was always interesting to watch operations. Class J68 No. 68643 prepares to commence unloading.

Belstead Bank, south of Ipswich, was a lovely spot to watch trains go by. Britannia No. 70001 *Lord Hurcomb* passes with a Norwich to London Liverpool Street express.

September 1951, B12/3 No. 61535 climbs Belstead Bank with a Cromer and Sheringham to London Liverpool Street train. Even when more modern classes were allocated to Great Eastern routes, members of the B12/3 class were often used on front-line services. For several years after Second World War, Stratford turned out B12/3 locomotives in unlined black. Just one member of the class received LNER post-war green before all were repainted with BR lined black livery.

Further up Belstead Bank, Class K3 No. 61834 is seen in the 1950s with a London-bound, Saturday extra, up express. The locomotive is one of the earlier examples with right-hand drive and an older design of group-standard tender.

Water troughs at Halifax Junction south of Ipswich. Class B1 No. 61059 nicely cleaned, with burnished buffers, passes with a London Liverpool Street express. On busy summer Saturdays there were several non-stop services using the troughs. If the troughs had too little time to refill between trains, crews would often top-up with water during an Ipswich stop.

Near Halifax Junction in the 1950s. The crew of Britannia No. 70005 *John Milton* are taking advantage of the water troughs just south of Ipswich.

Ipswich shed *c.* 1950; J15 No. 65461 stands behind D16/3 No. 62612. Unique for a slide-valve D16/3, after an accident near Clacton in 1931, No. 62612 was repaired with mainframes designed for piston valve variants.

Ipswich shed was a busy depot. Gresley K3 No. 61959 is waiting for her next turn of duty. A Thompson L1 lurks in the background; these tank locomotives were often used on trains to Felixstowe.

Pictured at Ipswich, soon after her introduction in 1951, is the first of the BR standard 7MT Britannia class, No. 70000 *Britannia*. She's fitted with the original and flatter dome design. A later steam collection modification reduced water carry over but needed a more rounded dome to accommodate updated components. The Britannia class took over principal trains between Norwich and London Liverpool Street, including some that were routed via Cambridge and Ely.

Thompson B1 No. 61050 arrives at Ipswich on 14 May 1951 (Whit Monday), with a Norwich to London Liverpool Street service. The mixed selection of coaches is typical of East Anglian trains in the 1950s. Seen in BR lined black livery, like many of her class allocated to Norwich and Ipswich, she appears to have been very well presented.

At the same Ipswich location on Whit Monday 1951, Class L1 No. 67705 brings in a Felixstowe to London Liverpool Street through train. The L1 will be replaced for the run forward to London.

Thompson B1 No. 61042 at Ipswich with a non-stop summer service from Great Yarmouth to London Liverpool Street. London-bound non-stop trains had the benefit of a through road. Non-stops in the opposite direction used one of the two down line platform roads.

Class J17 No. 65566 at Ipswich in 1951 with empty stock from Great Yarmouth. The train is using the through road for services that are not stopping. On bank holidays and summer Saturdays, empty stock movements were often necessary at the end of the day.

Pictured in the 1950s, Thompson B1 No. 61042 sweeps out of Ipswich tunnel. The first coach is a former Great Eastern Railway vehicle probably added for additional accommodation. On summer Saturdays the East Suffolk was a very busy line.

Thompson B1 No. 61045 was a hurried replacement for a Britannia removed before departure from Norwich. The crew made a valiant effort to keep up with the fast 7MT schedule. We arrived on-time after a spectacular run; the locomotive was worked hard with plenty of noise from the front!

Class J15 No. 65467 arriving at Felixstowe Town station with a through service from Felixstowe Beach to London Liverpool Street. The J15 will run-round her train for the onward journey, taking the train as far as Ipswich.

Having run-round her train, J15 No. 65467 sets out for Ipswich. She will be replaced by more suitable motive-power for the run to London Liverpool Street.

Class C12 No. 67360 arrives at Bury St Edmunds with a train from Long Melford. A short branch line connected Bury St Edmunds with Long Melford on the Stour Valley Railway. It was closed to passengers in April 1961 and closed to freight in April 1965.

Beccles Bank was a nice location to watch trains, particularly on summer Saturdays, when the East Suffolk line was busy. Gresley B17 No. 61611 *Raynham Hall* is climbing with a London Liverpool Street express in June 1951.

Class B12/3 No. 61514 storms up Beccles Bank with the 2:40 pm from Yarmouth South Town, June 1951. The locomotive was a regular performer on the East Suffolk, periodically allocated to South Town shed.

Winter in the 1950s. Gresley B17 No. 61665 *Leicester City* climbs Beccles Bank with the support of one of her class mates. On winter Sundays, when the timetable was unbalanced, double-heading was a way to get a locomotive as far as Ipswich.

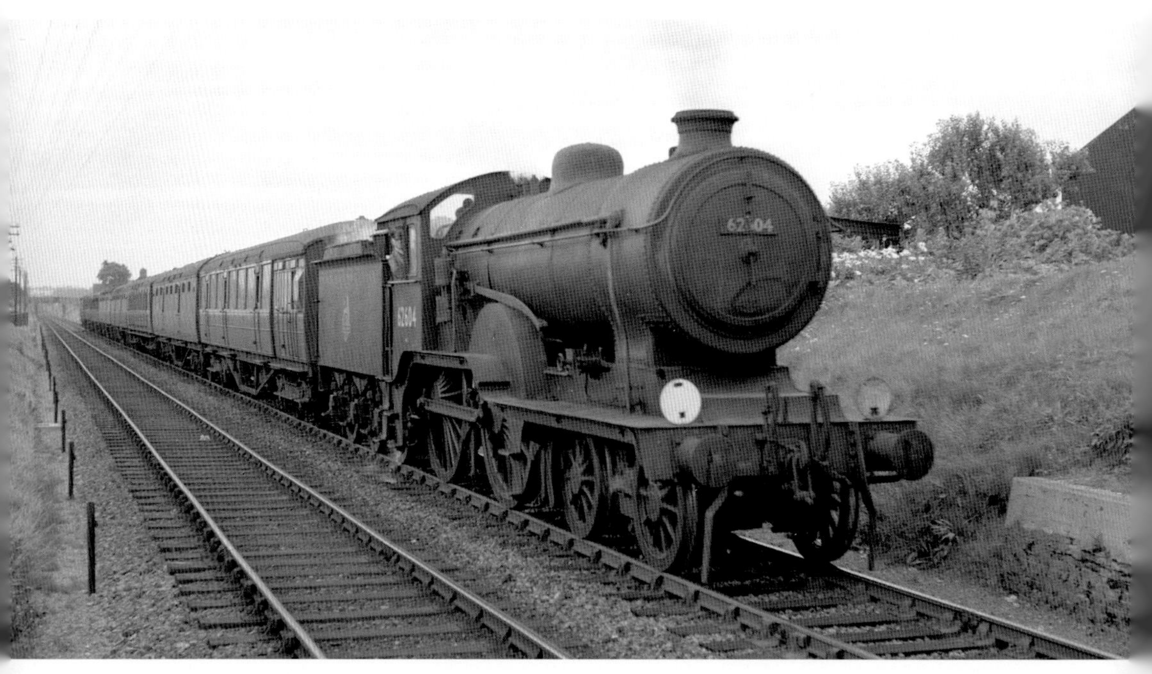

Carrying express code-discs in the Great Eastern style, *c.* 1950; D16/3 No. 62604 climbs Beccles Bank with a train for London Liverpool Street. D16/3 was the final of several related designs, fondly known as 'Clauds', after their pioneering ancestor Great Eastern No. 1900, *Claud Hamilton*. Designed by Holden and exhibited at the 1900 Paris Exposition, No. 1900 was named in honour of Lord Claud Hamilton, member of parliament and chairman of the Great Eastern Railway.

On 25 August 1951 a stranger attacks Beccles bank on a summer Saturday express for London Liverpool Street; former Southern Railway, Bulleid, Battle of Britain class No. 34065 *Hurricane*, temporarily allocated to Stratford. Several of her class filled in when newly introduced Britannia class locomotives were taken out of service to cure problems with driving wheels moving on their axles.

The East Suffolk line was a major route that was double track throughout. Today, there are long stretches of single track. In July 1957, Gresley B17 No. 61659 *East Anglian* arrives at Beccles, with a Great Yarmouth to London Liverpool Street express. The locomotive was one of two B17 class members streamlined in 1937 to work 'The East Anglian' express. Streamlining was removed in the post-war period.

Gresley B17 No. 61665 *Leicester City* leaves Beccles in July 1957 with a summer Saturday express from London Liverpool Street to Great Yarmouth. I remember that the train arrived a few minutes early which was unusual with the considerable congestion on summer Saturdays. Long associated with Yarmouth South Town; No. 61665 had her 'chimney to the stable'. Both she, and her crew knew they were heading home.

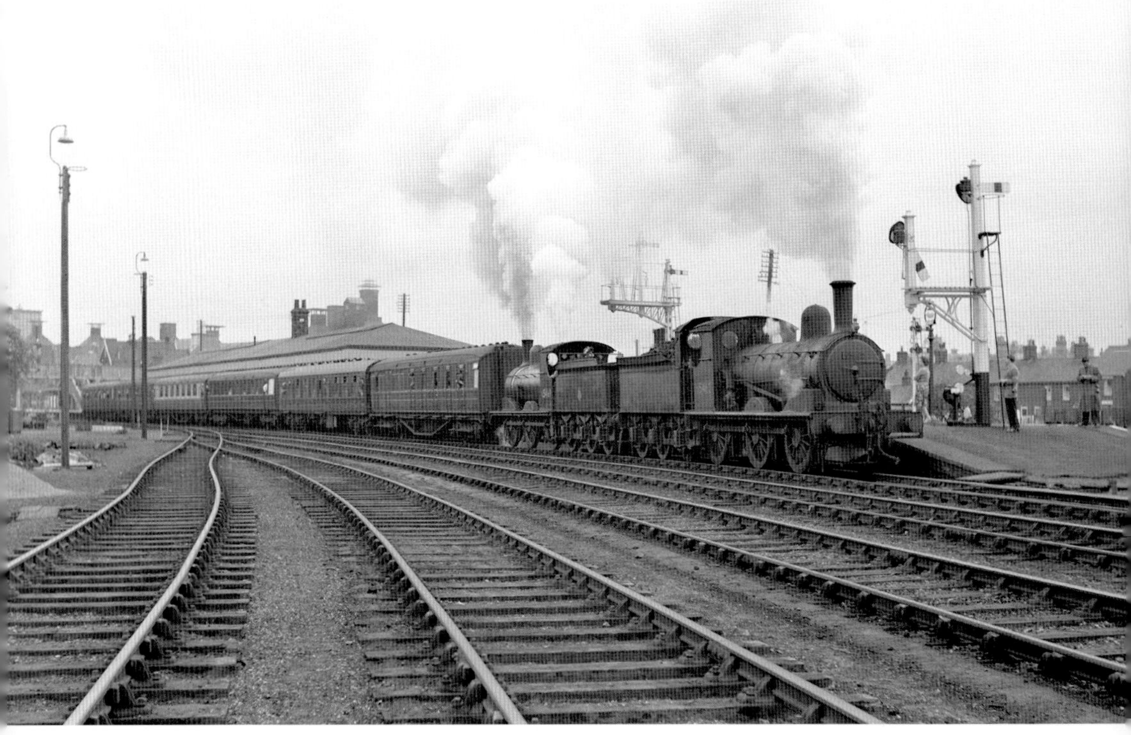

Beccles 21 May 1960; J15 class No. 65462 and No. 65469 double-heading a special train. No. 65462 was later preserved on the North Norfolk Railway at Sheringham.

In April 1959, displaced by diesel-electric power on Norwich to London services, the Britannia class were used more on the East Suffolk line. No. 70030 *William Wordsworth* runs through Aldeby with a Yarmouth South Town train. The Lowestoft portion would have been dropped off at Beccles.

Double-heading a Sunday train to resolve an unbalanced timetable. Bound for Ipswich, near St Olaves, D16/3 No. 62576 leads her shed-mate B17 No. 61661 *Sheffield Wednesday*. No. 62576 was one of the class members to receive piston valves when rebuilt to D16/3. Improved performance from piston valves increased mainframe fatigue leading some to be withdrawn early. No. 62576 was condemned in 1957.

April 1959, Gresley B17 No. 61611 *Raynham Hall* has just cleared St Olaves Swing Bridge on an up express for London Liverpool Street. The train is just about to pass through Haddiscoe High Level station. The lower level station serves the Norwich to Lowestoft line. A junction between the two routes was situated about a mile to the south.

Pictured in 1948, class D16/3 No. 62597, with help from her class-mate, starts away from St Olaves with a Sunday service; all-stations to Ipswich then, with just a few more stops, on to London Liverpool Street. Double-heading worked an additional locomotive to Ipswich to overcome unbalanced Sunday rosters.

St Olaves, April 1959, just eleven years after the smoke and steam spectacle of the last picture. Craven railcars have taken over East Suffolk local services. The station and permanent way still look tidy but closure of the section between Beccles and Yarmouth South Town is just months away.

Class B12/3 No. 61561 heads the 11:55 am train for London Liverpool Street from Great Yarmouth, on 2 June 1951. At this time the job was covered by Ipswich shed. No. 61561 would have worked down to Yarmouth earlier in the day.

Former Great Eastern Railway Class F5 No. 67199 leaves Yarmouth South Town with a local train for Beccles on 2 June 1951. These services were usually covered by push-pull trains. A possible failure has caused an improvised train to be assembled to run the service.

Seen in 1948, renumbered but still with LNER lettering, Gresley B17 No. 61601 *Holkham* rests near Yarmouth South Town shed. She is in typically poor late 1940s external condition.

16 April 1950. On the turntable at Yarmouth South Town, B17 *Holkham* is now in much better condition after a well-deserved overhaul. The fireman is Michael Collyer who I knew well. Like many locomotive men at the time, he had steam in his blood, and lived for the job. With the arrival of railcars, Michael reluctantly left the railway to pursue other interests.

Class B12/3 No. 61569 stands by the water tower near Yarmouth South Town shed. She has brought a train in from London Liverpool Street. Pictured in 1949, the locomotive is in Second World War unlined black livery, renumbered, but still with LNER tender lettering from her former owners.

Summer Saturdays were busy for Yarmouth South Town shed. Three locomotives, *c.* 1949, queue for the turntable. Thompson B1 No. 61236 has brought in a train from London Liverpool Street. She will return later in the day to her Stratford home; an out-and-back turn.

On 5 June 1950 Thompson B1 No. 61205 is at Yarmouth South Town preparing to leave for London with the inaugural run of 'the Easterling'. The service was non-stop in both directions between Beccles and Liverpool Street.

Yarmouth South Town renovation during 1952 and 1953. Ninety-three years after its 1859 opening, platforms were resurfaced, canopies extended, and a new buffet constructed. Work was suspended during the 1953 North Sea flood. South Town station was closed in 1970.

Nearly new, *c.* 1952, 0-6-0 Drewry Class DJ12 No. 11101 (later D2201) on the quayside beside Great Yarmouth Harbour. Diesel shunters replaced steam tram-engines for services along the quays at Great Yarmouth.

Norwich and Surrounding Branches

Thompson B1 No. 61254 leaves Norwich in the 1950s. This locomotive is one of the later examples built with an electric generator on the front of the right-hand running plate. The wall on the right of the picture was removed during spring 1956 to open a new platform.

Gresley B17 No. 61609 *Quidenham* at Norwich, probably *c.* 1950. *Quidenham* is one of the few B17s seen post-war in LNER lined green. The locomotive has been released after bringing a through train in from Cromer. During this period there were many through trains from Cromer, Sheringham and Yarmouth Vauxhall to London Liverpool Street.

Class B12/3 No. 61572 rests at Norwich ready for its next turn, a local service to Cromer, May 1961. Bill Harvey, the Norwich shed master, is standing behind the locomotive.

Britannia No. 70010 *Owen Glendower* stands in steam near the Norwich 'passenger signal box' during the mid-1950s. Built in 1951, it had a modern and effective Riddles design, Walschaerts valve gear and the patina of hard work and good maintenance from her Norwich home-shed.

Britannia No. 70007 *Coeur-de-Lion* at Norwich shed with the centre driving wheels removed for repair. Around the axle-box opening, the horn-cheeks protrude from the frames to provide more even stress distribution.

Britannia No. 70009 *Alfred the Great* temporarily out of service at Norwich with front bogie and trailing truck removed for repairs.

Austerity No. 90480 at Norwich. The locomotive is fitted with a Stratford shed plate. She had earlier been a long-term resident at March. Austerity class locomotives were occasionally used for freight services between Norwich and Whitemoor yard near March. Some members of the class were loaned to Norwich to haul concrete beams from the works at Lenwade.

Class J15 No. 65469 during her last days at Norwich. The shed master, Bill Harvey, had the chimney top cut-down and coupling rods painted red to resemble its former Great Eastern style.

Early 1960s. Britannia No. 70011 *Hotspur* stands close to one of the two turntables at Norwich depot. The excavator on the left stands ready to deal with the usual problem of accumulated ash. The coaling tower on the right was one of many cenotaphs, which they were affectionately known as after the famous London war memorial.

Thompson B1 class members No. 61204, No. 61205 and No. 61059 being prepared at Norwich shed for stationary carriage warming duties *c*. 1963. What a way to end years of service on the main line!

Britannia No. 70030 *William Wordsworth* and one of her class mates having boiler washouts at Norwich shed in the 1950s. The water softening plant at Norwich didn't supply shed hydrants. Raising steam with hard water after washouts wasn't ideal. As a local innovator, Bill Harvey, the shed master, installed a pump to make use of soft water left in locomotive tenders for initial steam raising.

Thompson B1 No. 61252 and a class mate on shed at Norwich in the 1950s. The new kind of traction, a Brush type 2, hides just inside the shed.

Thompson B1 No. 61254 at Norwich shed. The red stop-board, visible at the front of the B1, was used when somebody was working on a locomotive. One of the smokebox spark-arresting ash screens has been removed for inspection.

Class J17 No. 65567 being prepared at Norwich for a special working. Shed master Bill Harvey had given instructions for coupling rods to be painted red following Great Eastern practice.

This was the last regular run by a steam locomotive on 'the East Anglian' express from London Liverpool Street to Norwich. While Britannia and Class B1 made occasional reappearances, they were soon fully replaced on Norwich to London Liverpool Street trains by diesel-electric traction and, eventually, full electrification. Approaching Norwich, the train had an impeccable run; on-time throughout.

The triangle of lines around Crown Point goods yard. Britannia No. 70003 *John Bunyan* arrives at Norwich with an RCTS special from London Liverpool Street. The line heading into the distance leads to Great Yarmouth, Lowestoft, Cromer and Sheringham. An avoiding line behind the yard links routes from the Great Yarmouth direction with those from London and the Midlands. Much of the site was later cleared for an electric locomotive and diesel multiple unit servicing depot.

February 1959, Britannia No. 70002 *Geoffrey Chaucer* leaves Norwich. Immaculately clean, she has been specially prepared for a royal train working.

Saturday 24 March 1951. Before the introduction of the Britannia class, B1 No. 61042 leaves Norwich with the London-bound 'East Anglian' express. A twelve-coach formation was common on Saturday services.

Class L1 No. 67788 double-heading with B17 No. 61637 *Thorpe Hall* leaving Norwich, 3 March 1951. The 2:10 pm Norwich to Cambridge service was often double-headed because of an unbalanced locomotive working.

In the 1950s most of the local engines used on passenger trains were kept clean and well maintained. A B1 heads out on the Ely line passing under the Norwich to London Liverpool Street route. The two lines merge at nearby Trowse.

Trowse swing bridge seen from a freight-train brake van in May 1958. The bridge was replaced by a new structure in February 1987. The flag was used to signal bridge movements to river traffic.

With the introduction of the Britannia class, Norwich to London Liverpool Street schedules improved. Some trains via Ely and Cambridge were also hauled by members of the Britannia fleet. No. 70001, *Lord Hurcomb*, is beautifully turned-out as she passes Trowse with a London-bound up express.

Britannia No. 70038 *Robin Hood* heads to London Liverpool Street with 'the East Anglian' express. The train includes rolling-stock which dates from a special coach-set provided for the service before the Second World War.

Thompson B1 No. 61286 is going nicely as she heads away from Norwich. Cattle wagons were a regular feature at Trowse in the 1950s and 60s.

Gresley K3 No. 61877 runs through Trowse outbound from Norwich. Cattle wagons and pens serve the once-thriving livestock market. Animals were driven through the streets from the central Norwich market to join their train.

Nicely cleaned, B12/3 No. 61577 is London-bound at Trowse in the 1950s. During this era, many East Anglian engines were double manned. Sharing a locomotive between two drivers generated a culture of pride that was less evident with common-user allocations.

Gresley K3 No. 61921 storms through Trowse with a summer Saturday train to the Midlands from Yarmouth Vauxhall. The train has used the avoiding line, bypassing Norwich. Dating from 1845, Trowse was a terminus before the 1845 swing bridge enabled the line to extend to Norwich. Trowse station closed during the Second World War. Shortly after this 1950s photograph, many of the station buildings were demolished.

On 10 March 1951, No. 70000 *Britannia*, just two months old, passes Trowse Upper Junction with her first Norwich-bound journey hauling 'the Norfolkman'. The locomotive still has a flat-shaped dome-cover. A new dome, covering an improved steam take-off, was added early in the locomotive's service life.

Above: A long way from home, and close to the end of their life, former-GWR locomotives wait in Victoria sidings at Trowse beside the Ipswich main line, in 1963. Castle class No. 5099 *Compton Castle* in the company of 1400 class 0-4-2T No. 1473 and two 2-6-2T Prairie locomotives, No. 4106, and No. 4163, wait to meet their fate at King's scrapyard.

Left: A May 1959 view from the brake-van as a North Norfolk mixed freight climbs the bank from Whitlingham Junction, outbound from Norwich. Before brake-fitted freight stock became standard, brake vans were always present to help control the train.

February 1951. Despite her age, Class J15 No. 65478 is making good progress near Brundall Gardens Halt with a local train. With a nice clean exhaust, she's working well.

In the 1950s, the Thompson L1 class were used on some local trains in the Norwich area. No. 67795 passes Brundall Gardens Halt bound for Great Yarmouth. She would have picked up this summer Saturday service from the Midlands at Norwich.

Thompson B1 No. 61095 passing Brundall with a train for Yarmouth Vauxhall, August 1959. The locomotive is fitted with a coal-weighing tender. Used to measure fuel consumption, coal-weighing tenders were less tedious than the earlier technique of individually emptied coal bags.

Class B12/3 No. 61572 leaves Gunton on an evening train bound for Cromer and Sheringham, in May 1961, shortly before withdrawal and preservation on the North Norfolk Railway. Thanks to Norwich shed master Bill Harvey, No. 61572 had remained in service nearly two years longer than any other member of the B12 class.

With the support of Bill Harvey, the Norwich shed master, members of the Norfolk Railway Society hired a J15 for a day of driving and firing experience. Seen at Mundesley, on 15 May 1960, No. 65469 has had her chimney-top modified by Bill and his team to mimic an earlier Great Eastern configuration.

Shortly before her withdrawal from Norwich shed, as the last member of her class, B12/3 No. 61572 was kept in spotless condition. She was used on local services and special trains. Pictured in May 1961, she is being turned at Cromer Beach before a return journey to Norwich.

Left: Withdrawn locomotives were often used as stationary boilers, supplying hot water and steam to railway works. Class J15 No. 65466, at Melton Constable in the late 1950s, is fulfilling this requirement before finally being broken up.

Below: Pictured on 1 May 1958, Class J19 No. 64674 stands at Buxton with the daily freight train for Reepham. The signal in the opposite direction is clear but does not indicate there is a train heading that way. By this time, the signal box here was normally switched out and operated only when required. In this mode the signals would show clear for both directions of travel.

A small sub shed was situated within the triangle of running lines at Dereham. On a quiet Sunday in the 1950s, locomotives are simmering ready for Monday morning. At least five locomotives are present including Class D16/3 No. 62593 and J17 No. 65516.

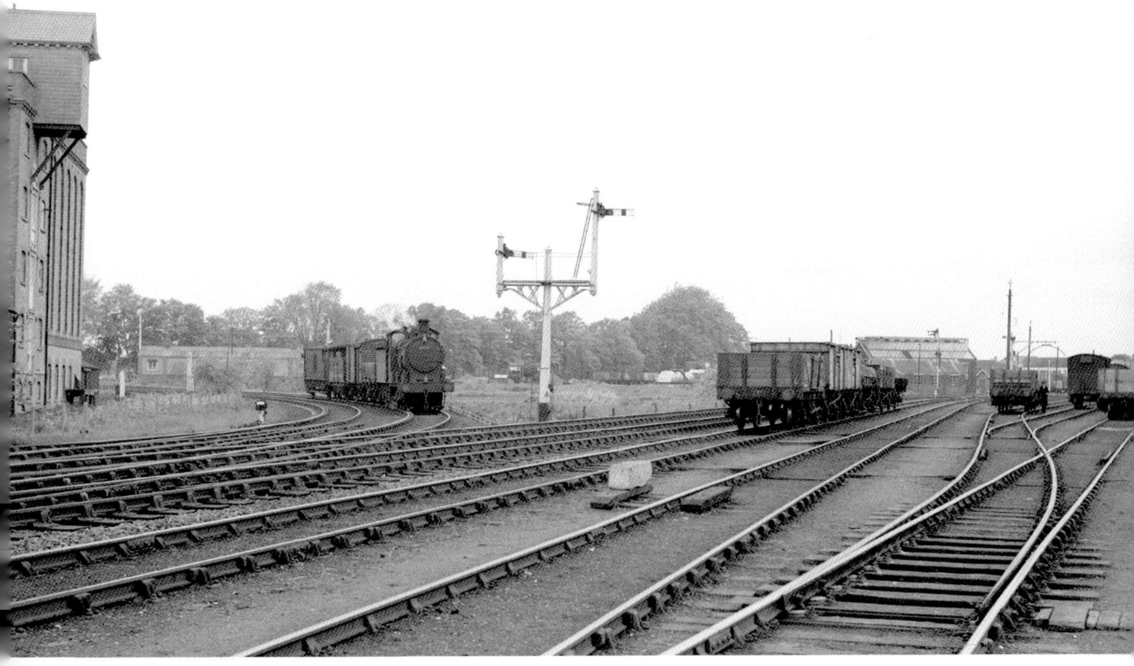

May 1958, Class J17 No. 65527 stands on the Dereham avoiding line with a short freight from the King's Lynn direction. She will continue forward to join the Wells to Norwich line. The route from Dereham station to King's Lynn runs in front of the trees in the distance. The land within the triangle of lines was shared between a locomotive shed to the north and allotments to the south.

Two Class J17 locomotives line up on their freight trains in the yard at Dereham. With three routes converging, and trains to shunt, Dereham was a busy yard.

May 1958, Class J19 No. 64644 is in charge of a freight train at Dereham. The train is shunting to the south of the station, and with busy sidings to the north, south, east and west, this could well become a time-consuming operation.

31 March 1962, near the end of steam in East Anglia, Class J17 No. 65567 approaches East Dereham with an RCTS enthusiasts' special train.

31 March 1962, Class J17 No. 65567 arrives at Swaffham heading an RCTS special train. The locomotive had been nicely cleaned for the occasion by the staff of Norwich shed.

Above: Class J17 No. 65586 is turned at Wells next the Sea having brought in the daily freight from Norwich. In the 1950s passenger-hauling locomotives in East Anglia were kept clean. Sadly, cleanliness was seldom extended to freight locomotives!

Left: A typical Norfolk mid-1950s scene; Class J17 No. 65586 has worked a freight train from Norwich and stands by the small engine shed at Wells-next-the-Sea. Turned, she's preparing to take the return-working back to Norwich.

Seen on 16 May 1961, in the last few months of her service, Class B12/3 No. 61572 had become a favourite pet for the Norwich shed staff. Pictured at Swaffham, with a school special for Liverpool Street, she worked the train back later in the day and performed well on both journeys.

31 March 1962, Class J17 No. 65567 leaves Swaffham to continue her journey around some of the soon-to-close branch lines of East Anglia.

31 March 1962, Britannia No. 70003 *John Bunyan* waits at Thetford to take over a special train for London Liverpool Street via Ely and Cambridge. She had earlier worked the train to Norwich before handing over to the Class J17 to haul the branch line tour.

31 March 1962, Thetford. Separated by forty-six years, Class J17 No. 65567 was introduced to the Great Eastern by Holden in 1905. Riddles' Britannia No. 70003 *John Bunyan* was introduced to British Railways in 1951. Standing side by side, perhaps they are whispering about their fate.

31 March 1962. Released from her train, Class J17 No. 65567 waits to head to March, her final allocation. She was withdrawn a few months later but survives as a member of the National Railway Museum collection.

31 March 1962. Britannia No. 70003 *John Bunyan* waits at Thetford to take an enthusiasts' special back to London Liverpool Street. Unlike her J17 companion, No. 70003's short life would soon come to an end. She was withdrawn in 1967 and broken up by Campbells in Airdrie.

March, Lincoln and New Holland

A general view of March shed *c.* 1960. The allocation of locomotives included many former LNER types. The depot was also host to a fleet of War Department Austerity 2-8-0 and ex-LMS classes. Little remains today of the shed or the extensive hump-shunting yard at nearby Whitemoor.

March shed *c.* 1955. V2 No. 60853 is in the company of a BR standard 9F and a Thompson B1. While March shed supported some passenger schedules, its duties were predominately freight.

Class J17 No. 65576 looks at home as she waits on the outskirts of March depot *c.* 1960.

Hill J20/1 No. 64699 stands at March ahead of its class mate and a Fowler 4F. Considered one of the most powerful British 0-6-0 locomotives, J20/1 were originally built with Belpaire boilers as the Great Eastern Class D81. Classified by the LNER as J20, they were re-fitted with the Gresley round-top boilers after 1943 and reclassified as J20/1.

Gresley K3 No. 61887 at March shed in the 1950s. The pit on the right of the photograph looks remarkably clean for the period!

Another view of March depot in the 1950s. Gresley O2/3 No. 63967 in very good condition for a freight locomotive, possibly after a recent overhaul, sits nose to nose with a Fowler 4F No. 43876.

March hosted many ex-Great Central 2-8-0 locomotives. Caught in the 1950s, Frodingham-based Class O4/3 No. 63666 waits for her next duty. The O4/3 class were a modified version of the Great Central Railway (GCR) class 8K design. No. 63666 was built by Kitson & Company and purchased by the LNER after First World War service with the Royal Engineers Railway Operating Division (ROD).

Class O1 No. 63786 stands near March shed in the early 1950s. These locomotives were developed from Class O4. Class O4 had earlier been derived from ROD 2-8-0 locomotives that were built to the GCR class 8K design. Under Thompson's direction fifty-eight members of the O4 class were rebuilt to O1 with an LNER 100A boiler and Walschaerts valve gear.

Sunday activity at March shed in the 1960s. Gresley V2 No. 60830 is being moved by Drewry Class 04 No. D2237. Finished in lined green by the LNER, under BR ownership the V2 class were initially painted mixed traffic lined black. In later years most received BR lined green livery. This member of the class is fitted with modified cylinders and outside steam pipes.

Pictured in May 1959, *Britannia* waits at Lincoln to take over a northbound summer Saturday working. No. 70000 was the first of the BR standard Riddles 7MT class. Built in 1951, and withdrawn in 1966, she has been preserved and continues to run.

Before the Humber Bridge was completed, the LNER (and later BR) operated passenger and vehicle ferry services between New Holland and Hull. Paddle Steamer *Wingfield Castle* arrives at New Holland. Powered by a coal-fired triple-expansion steam engine, she was built in 1934 and withdrawn in 1974. She is preserved as a museum ship in Hartlepool.

M&GN, Great Yarmouth to King's Lynn

LMS-designed Ivatt 4MT No. 43145 arrives at Yarmouth Beach station *c.* 1952 on the M&GN (Midland and Great Northern) line. Initially sharing duties with a variety of former LMS and LNER classes, in later years the M&GN became the 4MT's line.

From Yarmouth Beach to Lowestoft a Class J17 heads over Breydon Water Bridge. Demolished when the M&GN closed, it was one of the last steam-era main line bridges to be constructed and one of the first to be demolished. Still in good condition (according to the district engineer), decking was used to make new glazing bars for Norwich Thorpe Station.

Leaving Caister-on-Sea on the M&GN from Yarmouth Beach *c.* 1950. Class D16/3 No. 62564 has been rebuilt with a round-top boiler but retains slide-valves and the Great Eastern style running plates. Echoing Great Eastern practice, the smokebox-door ring has been conscientiously cleaned.

Chilled air and sea mist heading for Caister-on-Sea in the mid-1950s. Class B12/3 No. 61520 leads a train along the M&GN. Several Class B12/3 locomotives were allocated to Yarmouth Beach shed and used on the daily train – for Birmingham – with a buffet-car.

With many single-line sections, the M&GN made extensive use of the Whitaker pattern automatic tablet catcher. The equipment enabled trains to exchange track occupancy tokens, while running through passing loops at speed. A permanent way trolley and its shed complete the picture.

In the early 1950s, a Leicester-based Fowler 4F No. 44034 arrives at South Lynn with an M&GN train from the Midlands. Although members of the 4F class did occasionally reach Yarmouth Beach, trains were usually taken forward from South Lynn by Ivatt 4MT class locomotives.

Fowler 4F No. 44034 runs past the engine shed at South Lynn preparing to take over a train from Yarmouth Beach to the Midlands during the summer of 1958. The new engine shed, destined for a very short working life, is nearing completion.

Ivatt 4MT No. 43144 rests behind her home shed at South Lynn waiting for, perhaps, one last duty on 28 February 1959. On this day, the majority of the M&GN closed and she was reallocated to Stratford.

On 28 February 1959, the day that the majority of the M&GN closed, Class J6 No. 64172 is turned at South Lynn shed. Members of this class were regular visitors on trains from Spalding. No. 64172 was based at Boston and withdrawn months later in 1960.

Nicely cleaned, Class N7 No. 69698 sets out from South Lynn on one of the last shuttle services to King's Lynn on 28 February 1959. London Liverpool Street suburban electrification released members of the N7 class to replace ageing Great Eastern 2-4-2T locomotives on East Anglian lines. This example is auto-fitted to operate push-pull trains.

Preservation Journeys

18 August 1968, BR standard Britannia No. 70013 *Oliver Cromwell* and former London, Tilbury & Southend Railway No. 80 *Thundersley* wait in the station yard at Diss. Despite a British Railways steam traction ban, *Oliver Cromwell* had moved under her own power from Carnforth, arriving at Norwich on 12 August. On the previous day, she had worked a special train to mark the end of steam traction on British Railways. Later in the week the engine was hauled to Diss.

Britannia No. 70013 *Oliver Cromwell* starts its 18 August 1968 journey to Bressingham. The railway bridge at Diss was a tight squeeze. The Scammell Super Constructor 6 x 6 KVN 860E, courageously doing the hauling, has also survived with enthusiasts.

Safely delivered and being winched onto her track at Bressingham. *Oliver Cromwell* gave footplate rides on a short 200-yard route until 1973 when she retired to the Bressingham museum as a static exhibit. She was eventually released back to the main line in 2004.

Class J15 No. 65462 at Norwich in 1967. She was withdrawn in September 1962 and subsequently purchased by the M&GN Joint Railway Society. With cladding and dome cover removed, the rivetted boiler is revealed.

After withdrawal and storage at March and Stratford, Class B12/3 No. 61572 was purchased by the M&GN Joint Railway Society in 1963. She is pictured in 1967 at Norwich shortly before being towed, together with J15 No. 65462, to Sheringham for restoration.

4 June 1967, Class J15 No. 65462 and Class B12/3 No. 61572, hauled by Brush Type 2 No. D5533, head to Sheringham. Pictured waiting for a signal at Whitlingham, the train included the London area suburban quad set and two four-wheel lightweight railbuses.

Under the ownership of Alan Pegler, Gresley A3 No. 4472 *Flying Scotsman* made several visits to Norwich. Arriving in 1967, she is complete with a modified second tender from Class A4 *Union of South Africa*. With fewer water-cranes and troughs available, increased water capacity was necessary for main line operation.

Gresley A3 No. 4472 *Flying Scotsman*, Norwich, 1967. Bill Harvey, the Norwich shed master, studies his watch as sediment is cleared by a timed boiler blow down.